Dinosaur Poems

D1744590

Compiled by John Foster

Contents

Acknowledgements

The Editor and Publisher wish to thank the following who have kindly given permission for the use of copyright material:

Sue Benwell for 'Dream pet' © 1993 Sue Benwell; Doreen Dean for 'That's what you think' © 1993 Doreen Dean; John Foster for 'Dinosaur dreams', 'The dinosaur's bones', 'The 'Thumbs-up' dinosaur' and 'The dinosaur in the park' all © 1993 John Foster; Judith Nicholls for 'Tyrannosaurus Rex' © 1993 Judith Nicholls and for 'I'm a diplodocus' © 1988 Judith Nicholls, previously published in 'Popcorn pie' (Mary Glasgow Publications); Celia Warren for 'Eggs' © 1993 Celia Warren.

That's what you think!

I made a model dinosaur.
'My name's T. Rex,' it said.
I ran to tell our teacher.
She laughed and shook her head.

'You must have been day-dreaming.
Models can't talk,' she said.
'That's what you think!' growled a voice.
Our teacher screamed and fled!

Doreen Dean

Tyrannosaurus Rex

I am the BIGGEST dinosaur,
my neck is as tall as a tree.
I am TYRANNOSAURUS REX,
don't touch me!

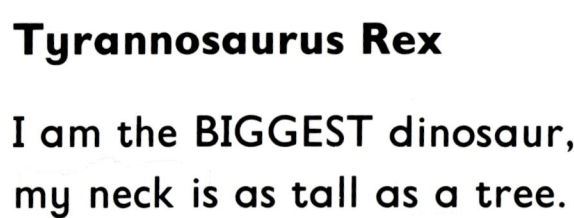

I am the BIGGEST dinosaur,
my body's as big as a lorry.
I am TYRANNOSAURUS REX,
if you touch me you'll be sorry!

I am the BIGGEST dinosaur,
my tail is as strong as a train.
I am TYRANNOSAURUS REX,
I am the King of the Plain!

Judith Nicholls

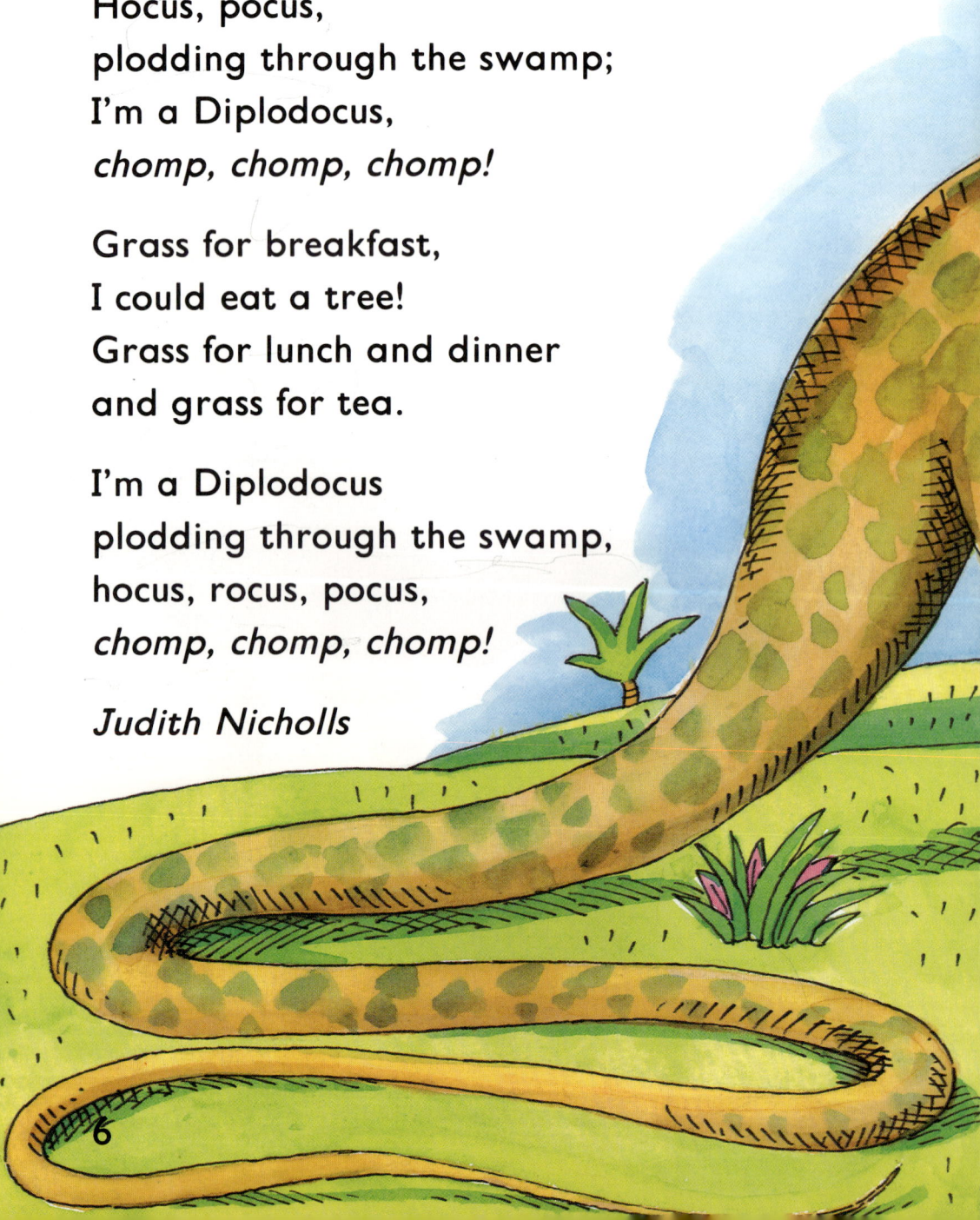

I'm a Diplodocus

Hocus, pocus,
plodding through the swamp;
I'm a Diplodocus,
chomp, chomp, chomp!

Grass for breakfast,
I could eat a tree!
Grass for lunch and dinner
and grass for tea.

I'm a Diplodocus
plodding through the swamp,
hocus, rocus, pocus,
chomp, chomp, chomp!

Judith Nicholls

6

7

Dinosaur dreams

Dinah Shore
dreamed she saw a dinosaur
knock on her window with its claw.

Dinah Shore
dreamed she saw a dinosaur
peeping round her bedroom door.

8

Dinah Shore
dreamed she saw a dinosaur
sleeping on the kitchen floor.

Dinah Shore
dreamed she saw a dinosaur
wake up and give a mighty ROAR!

John Foster

Dream pet

I dreamed I owned a dinosaur,
I kept it as a pet,
He really caused a panic
When I took him to the vet.

I shoved him in the waiting room,
A woman gave a shout,
The dogs all started barking,
So I had to take him out.

The dinosaur was so afraid
He hid behind a car.
The vet said 'You're too big to hide,
I know just where you are!'

Before the vet could calm him down
He'd galloped to the park,
His big teeth made a racket
As they chattered in the dark!

Sue Benwell

The dinosaur's bones

Dad said,
'Millions of years ago,
a dinosaur fell in the swamp
and died.
The dinosaur's bones
lay underground
and slowly, very slowly,
became as hard as stones.

One day, they were found
by a girl and her father.
Experts came
and dug up the bones,
then took them away
to fit them together.'

And yesterday,
Dad took me to see
the dinosaur's bones.

John Foster

13

The 'Thumbs-up' dinosaur

The dinosaur called Iguanadon
Had a spike sticking up from its claw.
That's why it's sometimes called
The 'Thumbs-up' dinosaur.

John Foster

Eggs

Each day I crack my breakfast egg
I hope more and more
That one day when I crack it
Out will pop a dinosaur.

Celia Warren

The dinosaur in the park

There's a red Apatosaurus
standing in the park
with a long ladder up its side.
We climb to the top,
stand on its back,
then whizz down its tail on the slide.

John Foster